MERMAIDS

MERMAIDS

COMPILED BY
ELIZABETH RATISSEAU

LAUGHING ELEPHANT BOOKS

MMI

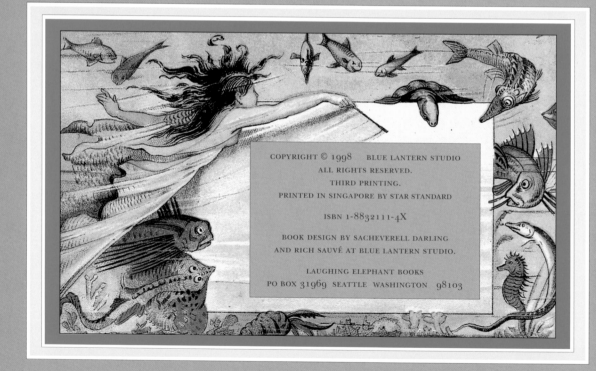

ISBN 1-8832111-4X

BOOK DESIGN BY SACHEVERELL DARLING
AND RICH SAUVÉ AT BLUE LANTERN STUDIO.

LAUGHING ELEPHANT BOOKS
PO BOX 31969 SEATTLE WASHINGTON   98103

MERMAID: A supernatural sea-dwelling female of general European maritime folklore: German Meerfrau, Danish maremind, Cheremissian wut-ian üder. The Irish mermaid, murduac, is Anglicized to merrow. The Morgans, or sea-women, off the coast of Brittany are considered beautiful, sirenlike, and dangerous to men. Mermaids are usually depicted as having the head and body of a woman to the waist, and a tapering fish

body and tail instead of legs. A carving on Puce Church in Gironde, France, how-ever, shows a young mermaid with lower body divided and two tapering tails instead of legs.

They live in an undersea world of splendor and riches, but have been known to assume human form and come ashore to markets and fairs. They often lure mariners to their destruction… Concerning the origins of mermaids, the Irish say they are old pagan women transformed to mermaid shape and banished off the earth by St. Patrick. A Livonian folktale says they are Pharaoh's children drowned in the Red Sea.

STANDARD DICTIONARY OF FOLKLORE: MYTHOLOGY AND LEGEND

MERMAIDS

[S]cience has not yet entirely explained away the mermaid who, like the Loch Ness Monster, still lurks on the borders of credibility. As long as parts of the world's oceans remain a mystery no doubt people will continue to believe in the existence of hidden submarine beings. Reported mermaid sightings while much diminished still occur, and the remoter regions of Scotland, traditional haunt of the mer-folk, have supplied several twentieth-century eye-witness accounts testified to with much apparent sincerity.

In an attempt to rationalize such sightings, science has produced a sea mammal theory reliant on the possible confusion between the mermaid and a surfacing sea cow or a basking seal. A lively imagination would be required for such mis-identification at close range, however, particularly in the case of the two favourite sea cow contenders, the dugong and manatee... A chance meeting between a dugong and a mermaid demonstrates the unlikelihood of mistaking one for the other.

BEATRICE PHILLPOTTS

MERMAIDS

In a somewhat simplistic way, a new quality was attributed to the Sirens, eventually becoming their distinguishing characteristic: eroticism. All their spiritual qualities have been passed on to the angels who, being immaterial and possessing a nature similar to the soul, were sexless, the Sirens became the agents of perdition through sex, and the bearers of eternal death.

MERI LAO

The conventional figure of the mermaid—a beautiful woman with a round mirror, a golden comb and a fish-tail—expresses 'The Love-goddess rises from the Sea'. Every initiate of the Eleusinian Mysteries, which were of Pelasgian origin,

went through a love rite with her representative after taking a cauldron bath in Llew Llaw fashion. The round mirror, to match the comb, may be some bygone artist's mistaken substitute for the quince, which Marian always held in her hand as a love-gift; but the mirror did also form part of the sacred furniture of the Mysteries, and probably stood for 'know thyself'. The comb was originally a plectrum for plucking lyre-strings... The myrtle, murex and myrrh tree were also everywhere sacred to her; with the palm-tree (which thrives on salt), the love-faithful dove, and the colours white, green, blue and scarlet... In English ballad-poetry the mermaid stands for the bitter-sweetness of love and for the danger run by susceptible mariners (once spelt 'merriners') in foreign ports: her mirror and comb stand for vanity and heartlessness.

ROBERT GRAVES

5

MERMAIDS

A frequent feature of the popular epic romances and natural history books, the mermaid gradually established herself as a distinct entity in the early Christian era. For Pliny the Elder, the fish-tailed women were a reality, living proof of nature's splendid diversity. There are several mermaid sightings in his Historia Naturalis.

BEATRICE PHILLPOTTS

MERMAIDS

In seventeenth century England... the existence of mermaids was as firmly established as the existence of shrimps. They were regularly seen off the coast of Britain, and travellers brought back tales of encounters with them from every corner of the seven seas.

RICHARD CARRINGTON

9

MERMAIDS

This evening (June 15) one of our company, looking overboard, saw a mermaid, and, calling up some of the company to see her, one more of the crew came up, and by that time she was come close to the ship's side, looking earnestly on the men. A little after a sea came and overturned her. From the navel upwards, her back and breasts were like a woman's, as they say that saw her; her body as big as one of us, her skin very white, and long hair hanging down behind, of colour black. In her going down they saw her tail, which was like the tail of a porpoise, speckled like a mackerel. Their names that saw her were Thomas Hilles and Robert Rayner.

HENRY HUDSON
1625

CHARLES ROBINSON

MERMAIDS

The moon is fully risen,
And shineth o'er the sea;
And I embrace my darling,
Our hearts are swelling free.

"That is no breeze's sighing,
That is the mermaiden's song,
The singing of my sisters
Whom the sea hath drowned so long."

JAMES THOMSON

A mermaid may appear in various forms. In size she may be larger than a normal man or smaller, but usually, she is the same size. Her tail may be divided or single, of medium length, or quite long and coiling like a serpent's.
She can change her forms, so she resembles an ordinary human, and live as an ordinary wife and careful mother for years, unless her husband breaks even accidentally some covenant between them. She will then disappear forever, sorrowing.

ELIZABETH RATISSEAU

MERMAIDS

A mermaid found a swimming lad,
Picked him for her own,
Pressed her body to his body,
Laughed; and plunging down
Forgot in cruel happiness
That even lovers drown.

W.B. YEATS

The natural history of mermaids cannot be understood by the methods of natural science alone. These hauntingly beautiful goddesses of the sea, full of mystery and danger, were surely conjured from the chaos of the waters in answer to some primal human need. Their genus and species may not be carefully docketed in the Nomenclator Zoologicus, but their reality in terms of poetic truth is firmly established in the impassioned imagination of men.

RICHARD CARRINGTON

MERMAIDS

Fair her face, and white her skin–
Have you courage her to win?
And her wealth it far outshines
Afric's gold and silver mines.
She exceeds all heart can wish,
Neither rude nor tigerish,
But sweet as roses in a bower,
And graceful as the lily flower.

RUTH MANNING-SANDERS

Outside the palace was a large garden full of bloodred and dark blue trees; the fruits there shone like gold, and the flowers like burning fire, and the stalks and leaves were always moving to and fro. The soil itself was of the finest sand, but as blue as sulphur flames. A wondrous blue gleam lay over everything down there; one would be more inclined to fancy that one stood high up in the air and saw nothing but sky above and beneath than that one was at the bottom of the sea. During a calm, too, one could catch a glimpse of the sun; it looked like a purple flower from the cup of which all light streamed forth.

HANS CHRISTIAN ANDERSEN

MERMAIDS

You—Mermaid! Your sea-green hair and sin-sweet singing
Bewitch me.

ANNE MARIE EWING

I have heard the mermaids singing, each to each.
I do not think that they will sing to me.
I have seen them riding seaward on the waves
Combing the white hair of the waves blown back
When the wind blows the water white and black.
We have lingered in the chambers of the sea
By sea-girls wreathed with seaweed red and brown
Till human voices wake us, and we drown.

T.S. ELIOT

MERMAIDS

Wonderful lovely there she sat,
Singing the night away,
All in the solitudinous sea
Of that there lovely bay.

Once Mermaids mocked your ships
With wet and scarlet lips
And fish-dark difficult hips, Conquistador;
Then Ondines danced with Sirens on the shore,
Then from his cloudy stall, you heard the Kraken call,
And, mad with twisting flame, the Firedrake roar.

Such old-established Ladies
No mariner eyed askance,
But, coming on deck, would swivel his neck
To watch the darlings dance,
Or in the gulping dark of nights
Would cast his tranquil eyes
On singular kinds of Hermaphrodites
Without the least surprise.

KENNETH SLESSOR

MERMAIDS

I would be a mermaid fair;
I would sing to myself the whole of the day;
With a comb of pearl I would
     comb my hair;
And still as I combed I would
     sing and say,
'Who is it loves me? who loves not me?'
I would comb my hair till my
     ringlets would fall
Low adown, low adown,
From under my starry sea-bud crown
Low adown and around,
And I should look like a
     fountain of gold

 Springing alone
With a shrill inner sound,
Over the throne
In the midst of the hall;
Till that great sea-snake under the sea
From his coiled sleeps in the
     central deeps
Would slowly trail himself sevenfold
Round the hall where I sate, and look
     in at the gate
With his large calm eyes for the love of me.
And all the mermen under the sea
Would feel their immortality
Die in their hearts for the love of me.

ALFRED, LORD TENNYSON

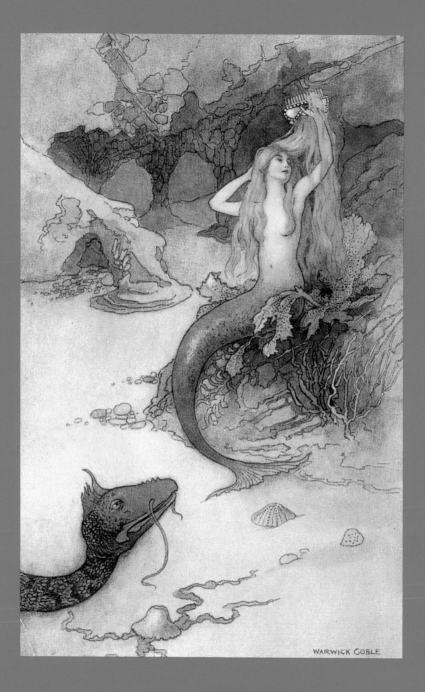

WARWICK GOBLE

MERMAIDS

Through many Mermaid stories runs a rather wistful feeling. Mermen seldom appear unless to woo the love of mortal maidens, and both Mermaids and Mermen seem to have an inextinguishable wish for something that can never be theirs. Many stories of the medieval period indicate that what they yearn for is a human soul… That is, though they are very long lived, they do die at last, and then they perish utterly because they have no souls. And in spite of the fact that Mermaids were often used by medieval preachers as examples of the false attractions of sin, it is plain that some of the Merfolk at least were able to make their peace with the Christian Church.`

GEORGESS McHARGUE

MERMAIDS

Now it must be remembered that the songs of mermaids have a charm compounded of water and air, the signs of impermanence. That is both their beauty and their danger. Many men have been caught, gaffed, reeled under and drowned by the lure of that song.

JANE YOLEN

MERMAIDS

And she sang a marvelous song. For she sang of the Sea-folk who drive their flocks from cave to cave, and carry the little calves on their shoulders; of the Tritons who have long green beards, and hairy breasts, and blow through twisted conches when the King passes by; of the palace of the King which is all of amber, with a roof of clear emerald, and a pavement of bright pearl; and of the gardens of the sea where the great filigrane fans of coral wave all day long, and the fish dart about like silver birds, and the anemones cling to the rocks, and the pinks bourgeon in the ribbed yellow sand. She sang of the

big whales that come down from the north seas and have sharp icicles hanging to their fins; of the Sirens who tell of such wonderful things that the merchants have to stop their ears with wax lest they should hear them, and leap into the water and be drowned; of the sunken galleys with their tall masts, and the frozen sailors clinging to the rigging, and the mackerel swimming in and out of the open portholes; of the little barnacles who are great travellers, and cling to the keels of ships and go round and round the world; and of the cuttlefish who live in the sides of the cliffs and stretch out their long black arms, and can make night come when they will it. She sang of the nautilus who has a boat of her own that is carved out of an opal and steered with a silken sail; of the happy Mermen who play upon harps and can charm the great Kraken to sleep; of the little children who catch hold of the slippery porpoises and ride laughing upon their backs; of the Mermaids who lie in the white foam and hold out their arms to the mariners; and of the sea lions with their curved tusks, and the sea horses with their floating manes.

OSCAR WILDE

MERMAIDS

Since once I sat upon a promontory,
And heard a mermaid on a dolphin's back
Uttering such dulcet and harmonious breath
That the rude sea grew civil at her song,
And certain stars shot madly from their spheres,
To hear the sea-maid's music?

SHAKESPEARE

A WEST INDIES FANTASY... The water of the Caribbean, iridescent, flashing from purple and green to infinite blues, dazzles and bewilders a Northern imagination. Surely somewhere in the glittering depths there must be creatures whose laughter shimmers up through the blue water...everlasting mockery smiling that earth's most beautiful boasts are less fair than the locked riches of the sea.

MERMAIDS

O, train me not, sweet mermaid, with thy note,
To drown me in thy sister's flood of tears.
Sing, siren, for thyself, and I will dote;
Spread o'er the silver waves thy golden hairs,
And as a bed I'll take them and there lie,
And in that glorious supposition think
He gains by death that hath such means to die:
Let Love, being light, be drowned if she sink!

SHAKESPEARE

The content of the [Mermaid's] song is knowledge, the threefold wisdom
possessed by beings who are not subject to time: knowledge of the past, of
the present, and of the future. Cicero stressed this, introducing the sirens
into his argument that the human mind naturally thirsts after knowledge. 'It
was the passion for learning,' he strives to persuade his audience, 'that kept
men rooted to sirens' rocky shores.' He then went on to give a free verse
translation of the Homeric episode into Latin.

MARINA WARNER

MERMAIDS

The waters... lead downwards to the underwater world, an idea found in all lands and the location of paradise in Celtic and Maori lore. Fountains, springs, wells, can be entrances to a magic world or to the realm of souls; they are part of the great feminine power of the waters, the waters of both fertility and death which sustain and destroy.

J.C. COOPER

The siren, who sings so sweetly
And enchants folk by her song
Affords example for instructing those
Who through this world must voyage.
We who through the world do pass

Are deceived by such a sound,
By the glamour, by the lusts
Of this world, which kill us
When we have tasted such pleasures.

FROM THE BESTIAIRE DIVIN OF
GUILLAUME LE CLERC OF NORMANDY

MERMAIDS

Leagues, leagues over
The sea I sail
Couched on a wallowing
Dolphin's tail:
The sky is on fire
The waves a-sheen;
I dabble my foot
In the billows green.

In a sea-weed hat
On the rocks I sit
Where tern and sea-mew
Glide and beat,
Where dark as shadows
The cormorants meet.

In caverns cool
When the tide's a-wash,
I sound my conch
To the watery splash.

From out their grottoes
At evening's beam
The mermaids swim
With locks agleam

To where I watch
On the yellow sands;
And they pluck sweet music
With sea-cold hands.

WALTER DE LA MARE

MERMAIDS

I turned and saw her: a smooth sixteen-year-old face emerging from the sea, two small hands gripping the gunwale. The girl smiled… this expressed nothing but itself, that is an almost animal joy, an almost divine delight in existence. This smile was the first of the spells cast upon me, revealing paradises of forgotten serenity… But she with astounding vigor emerged straight from the sea as far as the waist and put her arms round my neck, enwrapping me in a scent I had never smelt before, then let herself slither into the boat… from her arose what I have wrongly called a scent but was more a magic smell of sea, of youthful voluptuousness… She spoke: and so after her smile and her smell I was submerged by the third and greatest of charms, that of voice. It was slightly guttural, veiled, reverberating with innumerable harmonies; behind the words could be sensed the lazy surf of summer seas, last spray rustling on a beach, winds passing on lunar waves. The song of the Sirens does not exist… the music from which there is no escaping is that of their voices...

GIUSEPPE TOMASI 1887

39

MERMAIDS

Once more, once more
from Leucade's rock I dive
into the sea;
and once more
amidst the white foam drunk with love.

ANACREON

This music crept by me upon the waters,
Allaying both their fury and my passion
With its sweet air: thence I have follow'd it,
Or it hath drawn me rather. But 'tis gone.
No, it begins again.

SHAKESPEARE

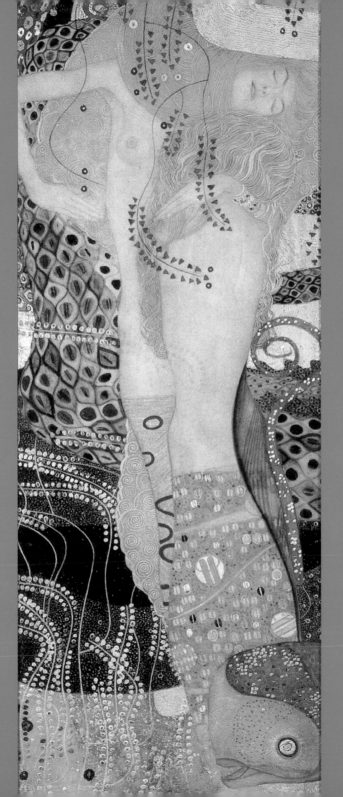

PICTURE CREDITS

PICTURE CREDITS

ACKNOWLEDGEMENTS

Sirens: Symbols of Seduction by Meri Lao, published by Park Street Press, an imprint of Inner Traditions International, Rochester, VT 05767 Copyright © 1998 Meri Lao. *Fairy Tales: Allegories of the Inner Life* by J.C. Cooper. Published by HarperCollins Publishers Ltd Copyright © 1983 by J.C. Cooper. Excerpt from *From the Beast to the Blonde* by Marina Warner. Copyright © 1994 by Marina Warner. Reprinted by permission of Farrar, Straus & Giroux, Inc. Excerpt from The *White Goddess* by Robert Graves. Copyright © 1948 by International Authors N.V. Reprinted by permission of Farrar, Straus & Giroux, Inc. *Neptune Rising* by Jane Yolen, published by Philomel Books. Copyright © 1982 by Jane Yolen. *Mermaids* by Beatrice Phillpotts, published by Russell Ash. Copyright © 1980 by Beatrice Phillpotts. We have been unable to discover the copyright holders of several of the works in this book, and hope to hear from them so that we can make amends and arrange to credit them in future printings.